Explore the Continents

Explore
AUSTRALIA
and OCEANIA

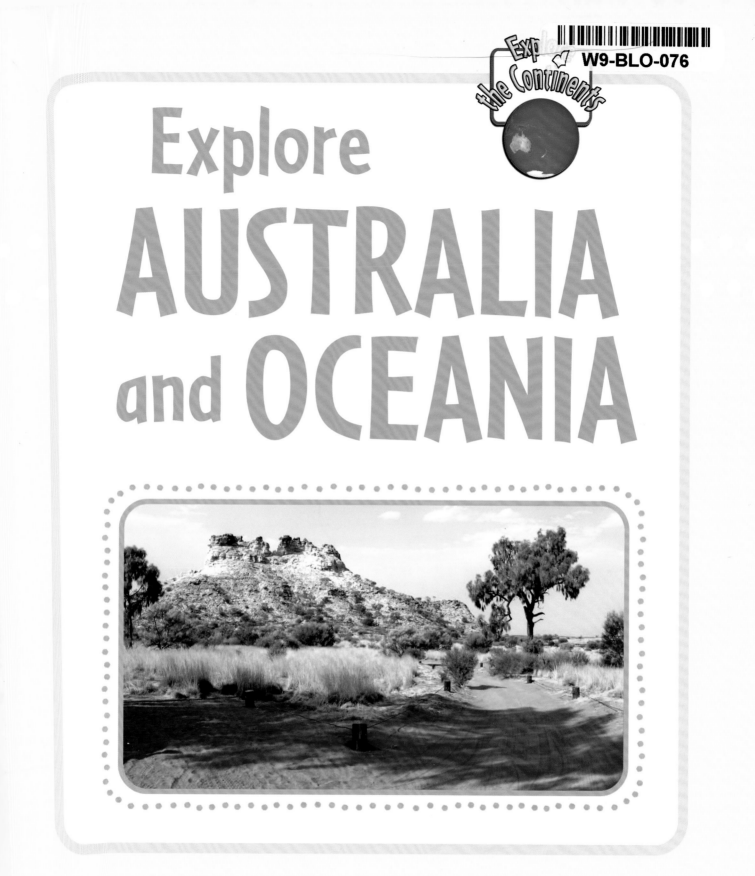

Bobbie Kalman & Rebecca Sjonger

Crabtree Publishing Company

www.crabtreebooks.com

A Bobbie Kalman Book

Dedicated by Rebecca Sjonger
To Jakob Malloch: Keep reading!

Editor-in-Chief
Bobbie Kalman

Writing team
Bobbie Kalman
Rebecca Sjonger

Substantive editor
Kelley MacAulay

Project editor
Kelley MacAulay

Editors
Molly Aloian
Michael Hodge
Kathryn Smithyman

Photo research
Crystal Sikkens

Design
Katherine Berti

Production coordinator
Heather Fitzpatrick

Prepress technician
Nancy Johnson-Bosch

Consultant
Dr. Robert Kuhlken, Professor of Geography, Central Washington University

Illustrations
Barbara Bedell: pages 10 (all except blue fish and map), 22-23 (all except map,
    blue fish, yellow fish, stingray, and lionfish), 28 (fish)
Katherine Berti: pages 4 (map), 10 (blue fish), 18 (grass), 22-23 (blue fish and yellow fish)
Robert MacGregor: front cover (map), back cover (map), pages 6-7, 8 (map),
    14 (map), 16 (map), 17 (map), 18 (map), 20 (bottom right), 22-23 (map)
Cori Marvin: pages 22-23 (lionfish and stingray)
Vanessa Parson-Robbs: pages 10 (map), 12 (top left), 20 (top), 24 (map), 28 (map),
    30 (map), 31 (maps)
Bonna Rouse: pages 4 (plant and butterfly), 8 (all except map), 19, 26
Margaret Amy Salter: page 21

Photographs
© Jo Chambers. Image from BigStockPhoto.com: page 11 (top)
Dreamstime.com: page 30; Ian Bracejirdle: page 11 (bottom); Ilya Genkin: page 5
Fotolia.com: pages 13, 27, 29 (bottom)
photolibrary.com pty.ltd/Index Stock: page 19
iStockphoto.com: front cover, back cover, pages 1, 8 (top left), 9, 12, 15, 24,
    29 (middle), 31 (bottom)
© Shutterstock: Robert Hoehne: page 20 (left); Styve Reineck: page 18 (bottom left);
    Harris Shiffman: page 29 (top); Eldad Yitzhak: page 17 (bottom)
Other images by Corel, Creatas, Digital Stock, Digital Vision, gemvision.com,
    and Photodisc

Library and Archives Canada Cataloguing in Publication

Kalman, Bobbie, 1947-
    Explore Australia and Oceania / Bobbie Kalman &
Rebecca Sjonger.

(Explore the continents)
Includes index.
ISBN 978-0-7787-3073-6 (bound)
ISBN 978-0-7787-3087-3 (pbk.)

    1. Australia--Geography--Juvenile literature. 2. Oceania--
Geography--Juvenile literature. I. Sjonger, Rebecca II. Title.
III. Series.

DU96.K34 2007   j919   C2007-900736-8

Library of Congress Cataloging-in-Publication Data

Kalman, Bobbie.
  Explore Australia and Oceania / Bobbie Kalman & Rebecca
Sjonger.
      p. cm. -- (Explore the continents)
  Includes index.
  ISBN-13: 978-0-7787-3073-6 (rlb)
  ISBN-10: 0-7787-3073-5 (rlb)
  ISBN-13: 978-0-7787-3087-3 (pb)
  ISBN-10: 0-7787-3087-5 (pb)
  1. Australia--Juvenile literature. 2. Australia--Geography--Juvenile
literature. 3. Oceania--Juvenile literature. 4. Oceania--Geography--
Juvenile literature. I. Sjonger, Rebecca. II. Title. III. Series.
  DU96.K35 2007
  919--dc22
                                                                2007003496

Crabtree Publishing Company

www.crabtreebooks.com   1-800-387-7650

Printed in Canada/102017/MA20170906

Published in Canada
Crabtree Publishing
616 Welland Ave.
St. Catharines, Ontario
L2M 5V6

Published in the United States
Crabtree Publishing
PMB 59051
350 Fifth Ave., 59th Floor
New York, NY 10118

Published in the United Kingdom
Crabtree Publishing
Maritime House
Basin Road North, Hove
BN41 1WR

Published in Australia
Crabtree Publishing
3 Charles Street
Coburg North
VIC, 3058

Contents

Looking at Earth

There is a lot of water on Earth. Most of the water is in **oceans**. Oceans are very big areas of water. There are five oceans on Earth. In order from largest to smallest, the five oceans are the Pacific Ocean, the Atlantic Ocean, the Indian Ocean, the Southern Ocean, and the Arctic Ocean.

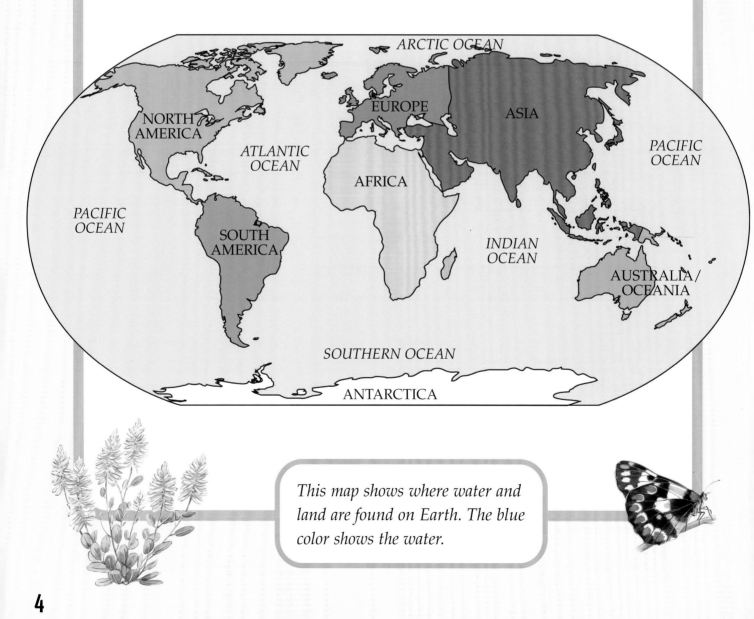

This map shows where water and land are found on Earth. The blue color shows the water.

Land on Earth

There are also very big areas of land on Earth. These areas of land are called **continents**. There are seven continents. From largest to smallest, the continents are Asia, Africa, North America, South America, Antarctica, Europe, and Australia/Oceania.

*This picture shows part of Australia's **coast**. A coast is land that touches an ocean. This ocean is the Indian Ocean.*

What is Australia/Oceania?

Australia is a very large area of land, so it is called a continent. There are many small areas of land around Australia. Tahiti and New Zealand are two of these areas. These areas do not belong to any continent. The part of the world that includes Australia and these small areas of land is called **Oceania**. In this book, you will learn about Australia and some other places found in Oceania.

The hemispheres

There are four main **directions** on Earth. North, south, east, and west are the four main directions. The **North Pole** is the most northern place on Earth. The **South Pole** is the most southern place on Earth. In areas near the North Pole and the South Pole, the weather is always very cold.

AUSTRALIA/ OCEANIA

N

W ← ⊕ → E

S

NORTH POLE

EQUATOR

SOUTH POLE

EQUATOR

Above the equator

The **Northern Hemisphere** is the top part of Earth. It stretches from the **equator** to the North Pole.

Two parts

The equator is an imaginary circle around the center of Earth. It divides Earth into two equal parts. In areas near the equator, the weather is hot all year.

Below the equator

The **Southern Hemisphere** is the bottom part of Earth. It stretches from the equator to the South Pole. Australia/Oceania is in the Southern Hemisphere.

An island continent

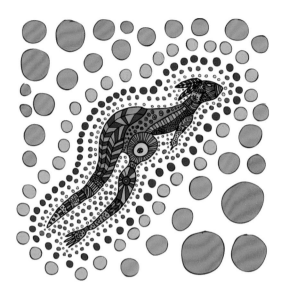

Australia is the smallest continent on Earth. It is completely surrounded by water. Land that is completely surrounded by water is called an **island**. Australia is an island continent.

AUSTRALIA

TASMANIA →

Tasmania

Many small islands are also part of the continent of Australia. Tasmania is a small island that is part of Australia. Tasmania is near the southern coast of Australia.

Animals called Tasmanian devils live only in Tasmania.

Fast fact

Tasmania is often called the "Natural State" because the land is very clean and not **polluted**.

Oceania

Australia is part of a large area called Oceania. The name "Oceania" tells us that the Pacific Ocean is a big part of this area. This huge area also includes thousands of islands. These islands are to the north and east of the continent of Australia.

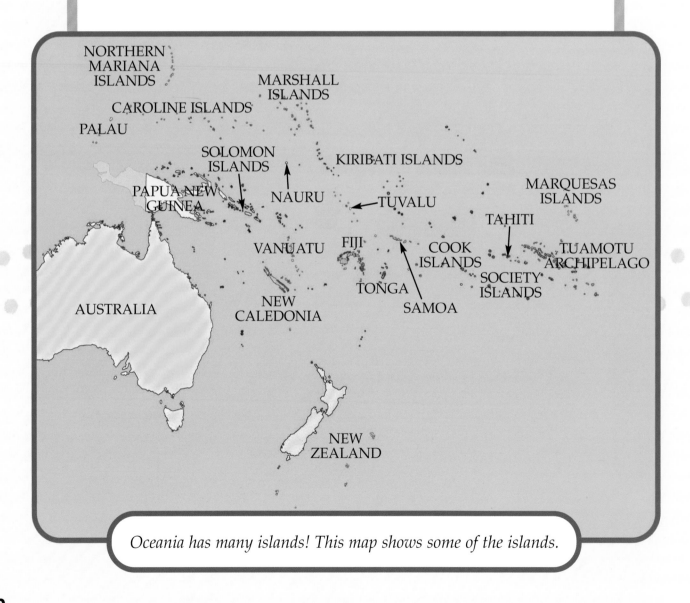

Oceania has many islands! This map shows some of the islands.

This picture shows a city in New Zealand called Auckland. Over a million people live in Auckland.

The islands in Oceania

Some islands in Oceania are **inhabited**. Inhabited means that people live there. New Zealand, Tahiti, and Fiji are inhabited islands in Oceania. Other islands in Oceania are **uninhabited**. No one lives on these islands.

This uninhabited island is part of Oceania.

Different climates

Climate is the usual weather in an area. It includes temperature, rainfall, and wind. The northern part of Australia is near the equator. This area is hot all year. Many of the islands in Oceania are close to the equator, too. They always have hot weather. Fiji and Samoa are always hot. New Zealand and the southern part of Australia are farther from the equator. The weather in these southern areas is usually cool.

Tahiti is in Oceania. The weather is always hot in Tahiti.

Dry or rainy

Most of Australia is very dry all year. Only the most northern part of the continent gets a lot of rain. Many of the other islands in Oceania get a lot of rain for half the year. They get very little rain for the rest of the year.

In Southern Australia, it sometimes snows in winter.

Surrounded by water

The western coast of Australia touches the Indian Ocean. The eastern coast of Australia touches the Pacific Ocean. There are also many **seas** around Australia. A sea is a small area of an ocean. A sea has land around it.

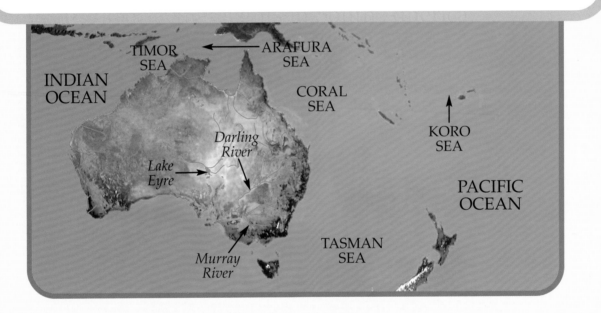

Water in Oceania

The Pacific Ocean surrounds most of the islands in Oceania. Some of these islands also touch seas.

Koro Sea is near Fiji.

Saltwater crocodiles live in many rivers and **swamps** in Australia.

Rarely filled

There are very few **rivers** and **lakes** in Australia. The longest rivers in Australia are the Murray River and the Darling River. They have water in them all year. Many of Australia's rivers and lakes are usually dry! They are filled with water only when it rains. The largest lake in Australia is Lake Eyre. Lake Eyre is rarely filled with water. It is a **saltwater** lake. Salt water has a lot of salt in it.

When Lake Eyre is dry, the salt from the water makes a thick crust on the ground.

How the land looks

This map shows the locations of some famous rock formations in Australia.

BUNGLE BUNGLE
DEVIL'S MARBLES
KATA TJUTA
ULURU
PINNACLES
TWELVE APOSTLES

Australia has many large **rock formations**. A rock formation is a big piece of rock that has an unusual shape. Rock formations are a kind of **landform**. Landforms are areas of land with certain shapes. The most famous rock formation in Australia is Uluru.

Uluru is one of the largest rocks on Earth.

Deserts

There are hot, dry **deserts** in the middle of the Outback. Deserts are places that receive less than ten inches (25 cm) of rain each year. Australia's largest desert is the Great Victoria Desert.

The Outback has the world's longest straight roads.

Huge forests

Eucalyptus forests grow in Australia. These forests are made up of trees called eucalyptus trees. About 700 different types of eucalyptus trees grow in Australian eucalyptus forests. Kookaburras are birds that live in these forests.

*Kookaburras make sounds called **calls**. A kookaburra's call sounds like a person laughing!*

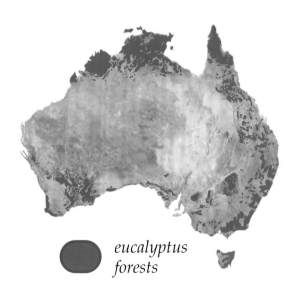

eucalyptus forests

Koala climbers

Koalas are other animals that live in Australian eucalyptus forests. They spend most of their lives in trees. Koalas have strong legs for climbing trees. They use their sharp claws to keep from sliding down the trees.

Koalas eat the bark and leaves of eucalyptus trees.

In the ocean

There are **coral reefs** in the oceans around Australia and many of the islands of Oceania. Coral reefs look like walls of rock. They are not made of rock, however. Coral reefs are groups of tiny animals. The animals are called coral polyps.

coral polyp

The Great Barrier Reef

The Great Barrier Reef is the largest coral reef on Earth. This huge reef is in the Coral Sea along the northeast coast of Australia. The Great Barrier Reef is about 1,400 miles (2253 km) long!

Great Barrier Reef

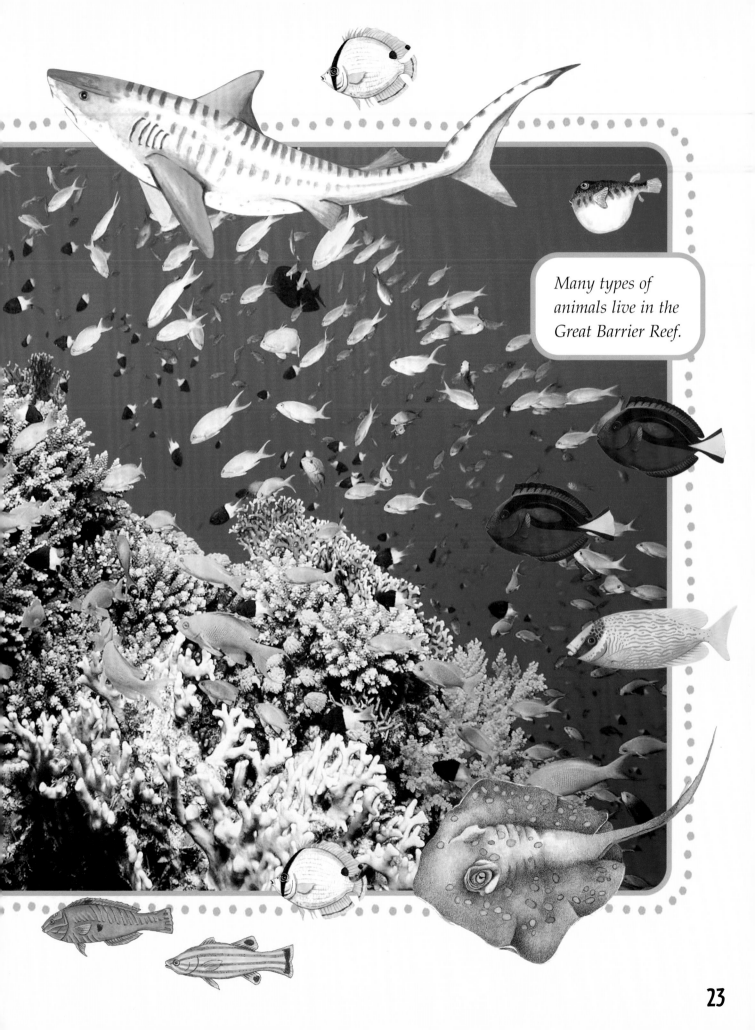

Many types of
animals live in the
Great Barrier Reef.

Urban life

About twenty million people live in Australia. Most Australians live in cities and towns. Cities and towns are **urban areas**. Many of Australia's urban areas are along coasts. Sydney, Melbourne, Perth, and Brisbane are four large cities in Australia. These cities are all found along the coast of Australia.

Sydney is the largest city in Australia. About four million people live there.

This picture shows the city of Wellington in New Zealand.

Living in New Zealand

Most people in New Zealand also live in urban areas. New Zealand is made up of two large islands and many small islands. The two large islands are North Island and South Island. The largest city in New Zealand is Auckland. It is on North Island. Other large cities on North Island are Wellington and Hamilton. Christchurch is a large city on South Island.

Rural life

Most of Australia is **rural**. A rural area is an area that is outside a city or a town. The Outback is rural. Some Australians live in rural areas. Many of them raise **cattle** and sheep on **ranches**. A ranch is a farm where one kind of animal is raised. In Australia, ranches are called **stations**. There are many cattle stations and sheep stations in Australia.

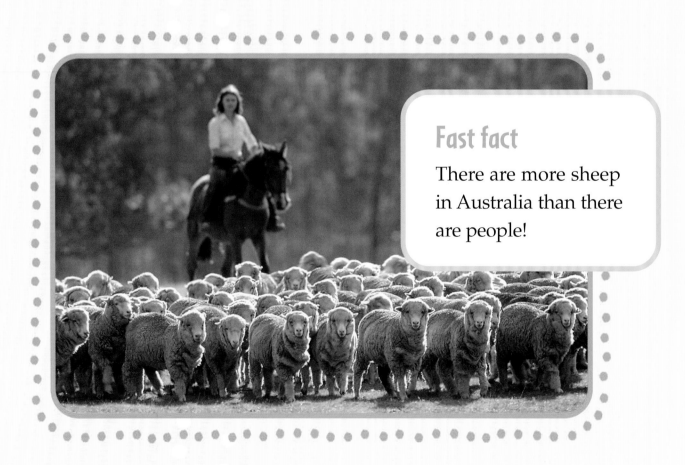

Fast fact

There are more sheep in Australia than there are people!

Village cultures

Most of the people who live in Oceania live in rural areas. Many people in Papua New Guinea live in **villages**. Villages are small groups of homes. The people in many villages have their own languages and **cultures**. Culture is the beliefs and the ways of life of a group of people. Dances, art, songs, costumes, and ways of celebrating are all parts of culture.

These people live in a village in Papua New Guinea. They have their own language and culture.

Materials from nature

Every continent has **natural resources**. A natural resource is a material, such as **timber**, which is found in nature. People sell natural resources to make money. Australia has many natural resources. Australia's resources include gold, **iron ore**, and coal. People dig these natural resources out of the ground.

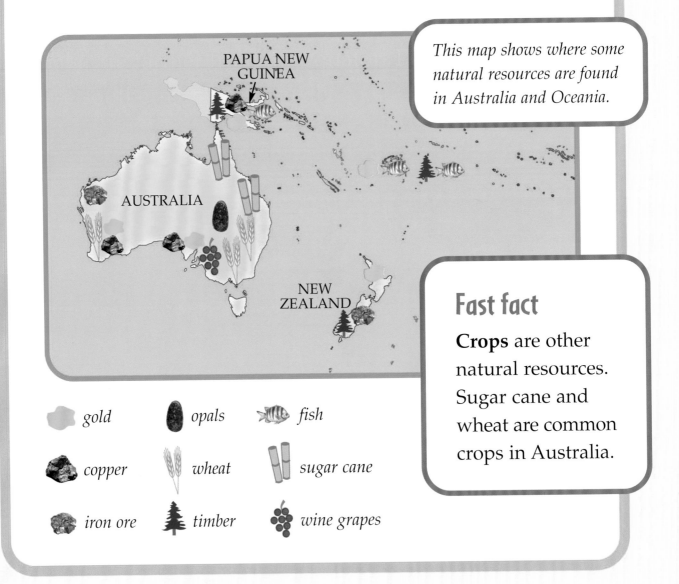

This map shows where some natural resources are found in Australia and Oceania.

gold   opals   fish

copper   wheat   sugar cane

iron ore   timber   wine grapes

Fast fact

Crops are other natural resources. Sugar cane and wheat are common crops in Australia.

Mining opals

Most of the world's **opals** come from Australia. Opals are **valuable** stones used mainly to make jewelry. People dig opals out of **mines**. Mines are large underground tunnels.

opal

This picture shows a place where people dig up opals from mines in Australia.

*Australia sells its natural resources to many countries. The resources are packed into **containers**. The containers are sent to the countries on huge ships.*

Postcards from Australia/Oceania

Each year, millions of **tourists** visit Australia and other islands in Oceania. Tourists are people who travel to places for fun. Some fun places to visit in Australia and Oceania are shown on these pages.

*New Zealand has many **geysers**. Geysers are columns of hot water that shoot out of the ground and into the air. This is Pohutu Geyser in New Zealand.*

Sydney Opera House in Australia is famous for its sail-shaped roof.

The Twelve Apostles are a wonderful sight! They are rock formations near Melbourne, Australia. Wind and water wore down the rocks until they were separated from the coast.

Glossary

Note: Boldfaced words that are defined in the text may not appear in the glossary.

cattle Cows and oxen that people raise for their meat, milk, or hides

container A large metal box that is used to move goods

crops Plants that people grow for food

eucalyptus forest A forest in which many eucalyptus trees grow

iron ore Rocks that contain a metal called iron

lake A large area of water that is surrounded by land

polluted Describes an area that people have made unclean by adding garbage or other waste

river A large area of water that flows into an ocean, a lake, or another river

swamp An area of wet land that has trees growing in it

timber Wood that is cut and prepared so that people can use it to build things

valuable Describes something that is worth a lot of money or that is treasured by people

wild Describes animals that live in areas that are not controlled by people

Index